How To Re(
2 books in 1

Copyright © 2016 HTeBooks

Copyright © 2016 HTeBooks

All rights reserved. This book or any portion thereof may not be reproduced or used in any manner whatsoever without the express written permission of the publisher except for the use of brief quotations in a book review.

Disclaimer

This book is designed to provide condensed information. It is not intended to reprint all the information that is otherwise available, but instead to complement, amplify and supplement other texts. You are urged to read all the available material, learn as much as possible and tailor the information to your individual needs.

Every effort has been made to make this book as complete and as accurate as possible. However, there may be mistakes, both typographical and in content. Therefore, this text should be used only as a general guide and not as the ultimate source of information. The purpose of this book is to educate.

The author or the publisher shall have neither liability nor responsibility to any person or entity with respect to any loss or damage caused, or alleged to have been caused, directly or indirectly, by the information contained in this book.

Table of Contents

HOW TO GET COOL THINGS FOR FREE 6

THE INTERNET OF FREEBIES: UNDERSTANDING THE MENTALITY OF FREE THINGS ON THE INTERNET 7

THE ULTIMATE FREEBIE STRATEGY 9

THE REVERSE PSYCHOLOGY TACTIC: COMPLAINING YOUR WAY TO FREE PRODUCTS 12

THE HIGH-END FREEBIE GUIDE: HOW TO GET AMAZING 'DEBUT ITEMS' AND HIGH-END SERVICES FOR FREE 15

MORE WAYS TO GET FREE STUFF ONLINE 18

FIVE PLACES TO GET YOU STARTED ON YOUR FREEBIE QUEST 22

HOW TO APPLY WHAT YOU'VE LEARNED 25

HOW TO HUNT FOR HIGH QUALITY FREEBIE PRODUCTS AND SERVICES ONLINE 26

EVERYTHING YOU NEED TO KNOW ABOUT FREEBIE PRODUCTS AND SERVICES ONLINE 27

HOW TO GET FREE STUFF FROM AMAZON 35

GET COMPANIES TO SEND YOU FREEBIES 38

HOW TO SCORE HIGH QUALITY FREEBIES ONLINE 44

HOW TO APPLY WHAT YOU'VE LEARNED? 49

How To Get Cool Things For Free

Have you been wondering why your friends are always boasting about how they get the best deals and even sometimes get free stuff? Do you ever want to know where they get all these nice deals from when the only thing you get is "buy 4 get one free"? Free things are hard to come by; nonetheless, this doesn't mean that they don't exist.

With the growth of the internet, everything is possible now thanks to the manner in which it (the internet) has made the world a global village. So, does that mean that hunting for deals online is as easy as abc? Well, certainly not; you need to learn the basics and master the art if you are to fully derive the most from your efforts.

This book will teach you everything you need to know to know about where to get free stuff online.

The Internet Of Freebies: Understanding The Mentality Of Free Things On The Internet

"People go back to the stuff that doesn't cost a lot of money and the stuff that you don't have to hand money to over and over again. Stuff that you get for free, stuff that your older brother gives you, stuff that you can get out of the local library."

-Frank Black

Looting the internet of all the free things it has to offer is all good and dandy. However, you cannot get free things until you understand why companies and other institutions offer free things. The internet of free things is not that different from a free for all sample galore. Whether you are looking for product samples or some services you have been dying to try, the internet has it all. What does this mean? Let us examine a hypothetical scenario.

Think of the internet as a trade show fair. In this trade show fair, there are thousands of companies and establishments trying to capture the attention of the visitors; in this case, you. These companies will go to great lengths to capture and hold your attention. At one end of these lengths is offering you free samples of their products and services. This in itself is the simple inner workings of the internet of freebies.

While this is the simplest possible explanation, there is more to it than that. What do I mean? Let us go back to our 'internet trade fair instance' for a while. We can talk for hours about using freebies as a marketing tool. In fact, if I was a marketing expert (which I am not), I would go as far as to say that freebies are the ultimate marketing strategy (who does not love free things). Well, this is besides the point and the reason we are here. One of the main reasons why businesses use freebies across the internet is so that they can reach a wider demographic, get feedback (positive and negative) on their products and services, attract new clients and most importantly, use the feedback they get to improve their products and services.

You should note something of substantial importance while on your journey to snagging internet freebies; the internet of free things will not turn you into a millionaire. Furthermore, do not be tempted to think that a brand like Apple will send you the latest model of their iPhone as a freebie.

In the internet of freebies, it is important to keep your expectations in check. While the above could not be any truer, it is also well to understand that the internet has no freebie limit. What does this mean? This simply means that with a little effort and ingenuity, there is no reason as to why Apple should be wary of sending you that 'new to hit the market iDevice' (we shall look at how to achieve this shortly).

Another thing you should note, and this stems from the $39 experiment: the internet of freebies is very eager to indulge your freebie whims. (The $39 experiment is the ultimate freebie strategy instigated by one Tom Locke).

Now that we have a general understanding of the internet of freebies, it is only fair to look at how best to cast our nets in this wide and rich sea of freebies.

*Key point/action step

All of us love free stuff. Actually, businesses have no choice but to give free stuff if they are to be heard, seen, known and even acknowledged. As such, everyone in the freebie business is in it to benefit in some way.

The Ultimate Freebie Strategy

"In any moment of decision, the best thing you can do is the right thing, the next best thing is the wrong thing, and the worst thing you can do is nothing."

- Theodore Roosevelt

Tom Locke's 39-dollar experiment

Getting free things on and off the internet is indeed not easy if you do not know which strategy to use, and where to look. In getting free things, the correct strategy is more like what butter is to bread i.e. very important. When I first heard about the $39 experiment by Tom Locke, I thought it was some clandestine method of getting freebies from companies. Now, if you are anything like me, you are very interested in learning exactly what this strategy is. To be brutally honest with you, the $39 experiment is not so much a strategy. It is exactly what the name says: an experiment. Let me explain myself before you get lost or confused.

In my view, the best way to explain what the $39 experiment is and why it is simply the best strategy to getting free things, is to use the view point of Tom Locke. If we were to go by the viewpoint of the genius behind this killer strategy, we would say that like most other innovation, the $39 experiment happened by chance. At first, this sounds very ambiguous, but the mystery behind it will easily dissipate once you hear the story of Tom Locke.

One day, Tom Locke was sitting at his work desk going through his unpaid bills. While looking over the pile, he stumbled on an unopened roll of stamps with a cost of $39 dollars. At that moment, he says that he thought what a joke $39 for stamps was. On the other hand, the $39 for a roll of stamps caused him to reflect on how much (or lack thereof) you can get for $39. Now, like I said, I am no marketing expert and I have no real tangible information on what $39 can or cannot buy for you. However, if inflation is any indicator, it is ok to say that there is very little you can buy for $39. This sounds all good and fine but it does not clear up the question of why the $39 experiment is in my view the best strategy for getting companies to get you free stuff. Not to worry; it will all be very clear when I tell you the rest of the origin story of the $39 experiment. Now, legend (I use the term 'legend' very discreetly) has it that after contemplating on the $39 roll of stamps, Locke decided to try something; something most people would not think of. He decided to take the roll of stamps, write, and send 100 letters to different companies asking them to send him free sample stuff. According to his thinking, doing this was no worse than losing the $39 in a casino. While I do not condone nor encourage gambling, you have to give a thumb ups to the Locke; his reasoning lacked nothing. This may seem a little off topic. However, the whole story serves a purpose; to show you how easy getting companies to send you free stuff is. To get free items, both online and offline, you have to use some ingenuity. The story of Locke continues. He states that his initial goal was to walk around the house picking up various items to get their addresses. I have to admit that in the vastly internet based social world that we are living in, this strategy of walking around the house picking up items is not a very good one (Which Locke found out because most of the items he picked up were all manufactured by a handful of companies).

So, how can you use the $39 experiment to snag free items online and offline? The answer is relatively easy. The $39 experiment is a freebie treasure map, cheat code, and compass all wrapped up nicely for your pleasure. How so? Well, what is the one thing you have to do if you want to get free stuff? The most important aspect to getting free items is reaching out. What do I mean? Simple. If you want free items, you have to reach out to companies (Hint: Tom Locke's 100 letters). Now, there is no guarantee that the companies you reach out to will send you free items. On the other hand, there is no indication that they will refuse you. You will not know until you take the first blind step. Furthermore, while the letter reach out method may have worked a few years ago, it may not work well today due to the simple fact that most companies have reduced their reliance on snail mail. On the other hand, most businesses are online today, which means, rather than opting to reach out using snail mail, email, and social media platforms are a sure way of reaching out. Furthermore, if social trends are anything to go by, every indication points to the fact that reaching out electronically will yield faster results.

For anyone looking for freebies, the $39 experiment is the perfect strategy and case study. On the other hand, if finding 100 company online addresses is strenuous, you may opt for a smaller number. If I were to give you sound advice, I would recommend that you reach out to companies you already connect with socially or via postal mail, or to companies that manufacture items you like.

Now that we have clear understanding on a suitable strategy for getting free stuff online, let us look at some other fundamental ways you can employ to get free items online.

*Key point/action step

Before you get started on hunting for freebies, you should perhaps determine what you have that will facilitate the entire process. You will be amazed by the value that some of the things you think are worthless can bring.

The Reverse Psychology Tactic: Complaining Your Way To Free Products

"Learn to say 'no' to the good so you can say 'yes' to the best."

- John C. Maxwell

At the core of our human nature is the desire for equal treatment. This underlying aspect of our humanity also translates to the items we buy. What does this mean? It simply means that we want to receive value for the money we spent on any products or services we purchase. If an item or service does not live up to its billing and your expectations, it is your solemn right to complain. Albeit being a somewhat fraudulent way of getting free stuff online and offline (unless you have a genuine complaint), complaining to get free items and services works like a charm, repeatedly. To any consumer friendly company or firm, feedback, whether positive or negative, is somewhat of a quality check. Do not construe this to mean that you should whip up your notepad and send thousands of emails complaining of everything. If you do this, you risk the chance of acquiring a serial complainer label (not good for your freebie endeavor). While I may not be a 100% proponent of this method of getting freebies, there is no reason why you should not try it especially if you have a genuine logical complaint.

There is a somewhat logical reason why complaining your way to freebies seems to work well. As I have indicated, most companies are consumer driven. This means that the companies will do all they can to make sure that the client (you) is satisfied with the services they receive (the value for money aspect). So, how does complaining get you free stuff? Well, companies take complaining as bad publicity and as we all know, bad publicity is bad for business. There is a simple way to looking at this. Let me give you an example of a hotel situation; if your soup has some cockroach in it, it is your right to complain. However, this does not give you the carte blanche to carry a dead cockroach in your purse or pocket just so you can get a free meal; that would be fraudulent!

There is a flipside to this. Remember what I said about firms equating complaints with bad publicity; it does not ring truer than with our hotel scenario. If we go back to that example, complaining of some uncooked food or hair in your food while other customers in the hotel are eating their meal is cause for alarm to the head chef and manager. Therefore, these two will faithfully move to calm you by offering to pay for your meal or offering you something else. For instance, they could offer dessert if you were almost done with the food before you stumbled upon the 'out of place' item in your food.

I also have to point something. Because of serial complainers, most businesses are very keen to get to the root cause of the complaint. This is both good and bad news. How so? If your complaint is fraudulent, the firm may press charges against you for maliciously tainting their name. On the other hand, if your complaint is genuine, the company in question will go out of their way to please you so that you do not take to the internet streets to air your complaint. End result=freebies.

Earlier on, I had promised to help you understand why complaining your way to freebies seems to work very well. The answer is pretty simple; the company is looking to buy your silence (and maybe win you back as a consumer). In fact, some financial sites advocate for the use of this tactic to get freebies. Additionally, by using the $39 experiment, you can complain to food manufacturers to get coupons or even complain to retails stores to get free items and gift vouchers.

With all this in mind, it is also important to note that the decision to give out free merchandise is entirely at the discretion of the company X (the company you are complaining to). This means that if the company has had its fair share of serial complainers, there is very little chance you will get a freebie regardless of the authenticity of your complaint. Perhaps of more importance to note is that most companies have a list of serial complainers (this means that if you are a 'free-for-all freebie-for-everyone' serial complainer, company X will simply send your emails to the spam folder or your mail into the recycle bin).

A good case study here is Ingrid Stone. Ingrid stone is a British national who gets goodies worth £2000 for complaining to multinationals. Ingrid does not consider herself a serial complainer albeit having sent over 1000 letters. In fact, Ingrid says that she only complains to those companies that offer her bad service. She does not do it for the freebies (although the freebies are a motivation). For example, after a train she was waiting to travel on was late, Ingrid complained to Richard Branson the Virgin boss, and got his signed biography as a freebie.

Lesson: If you have a genuine complaint, zoom through all the red tape and air your complaint to the company. If they send you a freebie, well and good.

Let us move on swiftly. What about when you want to get more high-end merchandise and services free? This will be the focus of our next chapter.

*Key point/action step

Complaining works like a charm in getting a company to offer something in return to "compensate" you for whatever "wrong" they (the company) has done to you. However, ensure that you only complain when there is something to complain.

The High-end Freebie Guide: How to get amazing 'debut items' and high-end services for free

"The most valuable thing you can make is a mistake - you can't learn anything from being perfect."

- Adam Osborne

At the beginning of this book, I mentioned that you should cap your expectations when hunting for freebies. I also told you that you should not expect to get high-end, state of the art merchandise free. This is true. However, there are some exceptions to this 'freebie rule'. Before I move on to explaining this, let me ask you a question. Would you like to own the next iDevice without having to pay for it, or get first class services without having to pay a dime? Well, I would and I bet you too would love it. There is a somewhat simple way to getting your high-end freebie. In fact, there are a couple of ways.

Review and blog your way to a freebie

By far, this is the easiest way to get high-end merchandise and services free. Why do I say it is by far the easiest way? This is simply because you get free items and services for giving your honest opinion about the item or service in question. For example, Cnet.com a tech blog/website gets many offers from multinationals looking to have their devices and electronics reviewed. Why? Because the firms understand that the consumer market is driven by information, whether good or bad (of course, company X expects a good review, but they also expect you to point out a few cons in the item). Because I am constantly writing, I might say that blogging is easy, more so, blogging for free items. The amazing thing is that in most cases, you do not actually need to start a blog to get free stuff. Bear with me for a minute as I explain. If you have used Amazon or EBay, you will know that these online stores have many under $0.99 items. What I have found is that most of the people who have listed these items (especially books and coupons) are always willing to give out the item to a select few in exchange for some form of review. In my endeavor to provide you with as much information on freebies as you can soak up, I should point out that if you want to get the cool stuff, creating your own blog is definitely the way to go. Other than getting free money from Google (AdSense revenue from the traffic the review will generate), you also get to keep the item forever; freebies do not come better than this. Well, the truth is that creating a blog and driving traffic to the blog is indeed hard and will require hard work on your part. However, like Cnet, once your blog is up there, the top brands (the iPhones, Samsung, Xbox's of the world) will fall over themselves to have you review their items. Blogging for free stuff is as old as advertising itself. Why? Because by giving you a free product to review, the company gets cheap promotion and advertising.

Mystery shopping your way to freebies

Sounds very clandestine, doesn't it? Mystery shopping is a tool that consumer products researchers employ to measure product or service quality. While this is the main scope to mystery shopping, it is much more than that. Companies hire a mystery shopper to purchase a product or service, ask questions about that service, make a complaint about it, and or behave is a specific way. The shopper then goes ahead to provide a detailed feedback report about the experience from start to end. While mystery shopping is indeed easier than blogging, the main reason it did not earn the tag of the best freebie method is simply because finding mystery shopping gigs is no mean feat. Additionally, you have to use your own money to purchase the item or service and get a refund later. On the other hand, once you get a reliable gig and client, there is no easier way of getting free things online and offline. The fact that getting mystery shopping is not easy should not dampen your freebie endeavor. If you are willing to put in the time required to go through the con artists masquerading as mystery shoppers agents, you are well on your way to snagging the coveted high-end devices and services freebies. What I love the most about mystery shopping is that just about anyone of legal age can do it (some companies also offer mystery shopping for teens). Another advantage to mystery shopping is that on top of getting your money back and keeping the item you bought, some companies go as far as to paying you an hourly stipend for your mystery shopping troubles; how cool is that!

A downside to mystery shopping is that it may take some time to build a mystery shopper profile that attracts those crazy to believe freebies. Mystery shopping is especially ideal for the freebie enthusiast who also loves a tinge of adventure. because, in most mystery shopping instances, you will be a shopping "James Bond" i.e. undercover. This means that if you create a reputation and an awesome mystery shopper profile, you could find yourself going undercover into exotic and exciting places (going to exotic spas isn't a bad thing!)?

Remember this: When starting out on mystery shopping, be very careful not to bite off more than you can chew. This means that you have to do some due diligence and sift through to find real companies offering this type of market research.

*Key point/action step

Although you won't ordinarily find high end items being offered freely in any website, blogging coupled with mystery shopping seem to be the ultimate hack to this. The more you work towards building a name for yourself, the greater the chances of getting more and better deals.

More Ways To Get Free Stuff Online

"Life is like a game of chess. To win you have to make a move. Knowing which move to make comes with IN-SIGHT and knowledge, and by learning the lessons that are accumulated along the way. We become each and every piece within the game called life"

- Allan Rufus, The Master's Sacred Knowledge

In addition to the methods stated above, there are a couple of other ways you can get some free items and services offline and online. Let us look at some of these ways.

Join a rewards scheme

This is also another cool way of getting some free merchandise and services. Most of the major companies and outlets have some form of a rewards scheme. What exactly is a rewards scheme? A reward scheme is a marketing strategy aimed at rewarding consumers for their loyalty. Loyalty scheme often times come in the form of plastic cards; i.e. club cards, membership cards etc. A loyalty card or program may bear different names in different countries. For example, in Canada, they call it a points or rewards card, in the UK, a loyalty card, while in the US, they call it a discount, club, or rewards card. While different companies and countries may offer different reward schemes model, there is some form of standard rewards methodology. In most of the rewards programs, you buy products from company X and while you are making payment for the services or item bought, the cashier runs your loyalty card through the machine and you earn points (most of these cards have a bar code scanner). When the points accumulate to a certain amount, you can redeem them for free services or items. Doesn't that sound precious? Furthermore, when you present your rewards scheme card, you are entitled to a discount (in most cases, a very big discount). This does not mean that you are getting a freebie, but it means that you are saving massive amounts of money while earning loyalty points that you can redeem for freebies later. In my view, you cannot go wrong with a rewards scheme mainly because rewards schemes are available for almost every pillar of your life. Whether it is eating out at McDonalds, banking or buying cloths at a mega store, you will find a rewards scheme. You can even join multiple rewards schemes; the more rewards schemes you join, the higher your chances of landing more free stuff.

I should also point out that instead of joining many rewards schemes related to credit card rewards, you should concentrate your rewards effort on one credit card to optimize your points and to make sure you do not draw yourself into debt. I should also point out that most of the rewards schemes available will require you to use your rewards points within a specific period. Therefore, you have to use your points once they accumulate to redemption status otherwise you risk losing the points.

Take surveys

By far, this is the most widely abused method of getting online freebies especially because many companies nowadays offer freebies after surveys. However, you have to provide a credit card. This is often times very bad because some 'fraudulent' survey sites are there to steal your personal information. On the other hand, you can use the following ways to separate the good from the bad.

#- Only sign up for surveys on company websites you trust (genuine company homepage).

#- Unless you are sure about a company's reputation (or website), never give out your credit card information. More specifically, never ever use your keyboard to type in your credit card info on these survey sites. Some of these sites use keyloggers that capture your keystrokes making it easy to steal your personal details.

You can also keep your purchase receipts after eating out or shopping out at a restaurant. I have found that most of the major stores we have today have a dedicated site where you can take surveys about your dining or shopping experiences to earn (win) gift cards, cash prices, or discounts on your next purchase. Additionally, when you visit your favorite company or brand website, there is a very big possibility that a pop up question asking you to take a survey will appear. Most of these pop ups will have a price at the other end of completion. Keep in mind that you should only use a trustworthy site.

In the same 'taking surveys for freebies' breath, I should perhaps also mention that you can also take paid surveys. Paid surveys are those that have a cash price attached. While this may not be free items, it is free money (who does not love free money). Many companies are fighting hard for your attention and opinion. Therefore, they hire marketers to conduct surveys. A quick search on the internet will bring countless survey sites (remember to be cautious) that you can try. Some of the more pronounced paid surveys sites are Survey Panel, Ipsos, and many more. If you are an online junkie, this is by far the easiest way to get free items. I have also noticed that in addition to the monetary value attached to giving your opinion by taking surveys, if you get a chance to participate in an in-depth survey, you can get products mailed to your home.

Trial memberships

If you surf the web for a bit, you will notice a not so new trend that is gaining traction i.e. trial memberships. Companies are using free trial memberships to woo consumers into using their products. I must also mention that most free trials are for non-tangible items i.e. online services like antivirus programs (Kaspersky etc.) and other internet based services such as Hulu, Netflix or Blockbusters. Getting free trial membership is indeed relatively easy. Whether you are a new user or an old user with a different credit card, all you have to do is signup for the trial membership and you are good to go. Most free trial memberships last anywhere between one to three months depending on the service. It is important to cancel your free trial membership just before the trial period ends or you risk the chance of paying the full service fee. Additionally, I have found that most of the daily deal website across the web e.g. groupon.com or dailysteal.com will offer you initial credit for simply signing up.

Use coupons

Coupons are the ultimate online and offline freebie deal; you can find coupons for literally anything; electronics, personal care products, household appliances, cosmetics, drugs etc. Although getting free coupons and matching them with their sales is a somewhat tedious process, it is definitely worth the effort if you plan well. Hunting for coupons requires dedication and some "tact" if you really want to save hundreds or even thousands of dollars a year by just redeeming the coupons at the checkout. You will be amazed to find that some items that are priced even $100 could be selling at less than $5 when you use coupons.

*Key point/action step

Getting free stuff is easy when you know what you are doing. You could find them in coupons, subscribing for free trials or even taking surveys. Whichever option you opt to use, you have to master it through constant trial (practice) to get better at it. Obviously, don't expect to save $100 on every purchase especially when you are starting out. Nonetheless, practice will make you better at what you are doing.

Five Places To Get You Started On Your Freebie Quest

"Education is an admirable thing, but it is well to remember from time to time that nothing that is worth knowing can be taught."

- Oscar Wilde

If you have been keen so far, I am confident that you have come up with a list of freebie websites and reached out to a few companies (remember that snail mail works best for reaching out to companies). However, if you are still not sure about where to get started, here are some unconventional places you can visit to get free stuff.

Craigslist

When most people hear me talk of Craigslist, only one thing springs to mind and this is online classified and sales. For this reason, very few people know that Craigslist also has an area dedicated to freebies. To access this section, navigate to the sale section and click on the free link. Here, I can assure you that you will find a wide range of items waiting for the right person to go pick them up (at the time of writing this, there was a 32-inch flat screen TV, baby cloths etc.). On the other hand, it is important to remember that the world is not what it used to be; it is now full of bad people looking to harm you (there has been some cases of bad incidents albeit a few). Be cautious before you go to pick up something from a person's home.

Freecycle

Freecycle is a peer-to-peer website where people post stuff they do not need and give it to a deserving person (the person giving away the items reserves the right to choose who he or she gives the item to). The main idea behind Freecycle is to render landfills (which is where most of the stuff you throw away ends up) useless. To get free stuff, all you have to do is apply for membership to your Freecycle local site available in your area. A great aspect of Freecycle is the fact that the platform does not allow for sales. All items are free.

EBay Classifieds

EBay is synonymous with auctions. However, just like Craigslist, eBay also has a very vibrant free items category with many items up for grabs (at the time of writing this, there was a baby crib, landscaping bricks, pets, and many more items waiting for you to claim them).

Freenapkin

Freenapkin has a lot of similarities with eBay and Craigslist with only one main difference: Everything on Freenapkin is free. As such, it is similar to Freecycle. While I was writing this, I stopped by the site and spotted chairs, kids play sets and car rims.

Barter Quest

Better Quest is a site that allows you to trade in something you do not need for something you need rather than buying it. Barter trade is the oldest form of commerce in the world and if you can make it work to your advantage, well and good. You may be throwing away something that someone else needs and is willing to give you what you need in order to get it. On the platform, there are no restrictions to what you can trade; all you have to do is agree with the other party.

***Key point/action step**

When you know where to shop/hunt for free stuff, everything else will be very easy. Craigslist, Barter Quest, eBay, and Freecycle could be a good place to start. However, ensure that you observe utmost caution if you want to stay safe.

How to Apply What You've Learned

Now that you have gained vast understanding on how to get free stuff, the next thing you should do is to start practicing what you have learnt. Start by deciding which approach you want to use in getting free stuff. It could be use of coupons, complaining to get freebies, blogging about it or simply reviewing the items, mystery shopping, taking surveys, subscribing for free trials/memberships and many others.

After deciding on which option to use, start learning more about it so that you are confident about what tricks to use in order to get even better deals. As the old saying goes, practice makes perfect; don't just learn about it. Implement what you are learning as you actually continue learning; this is the best method you can learn as opposed to spending too much time accumulating information when you could simply start. Your experience and my experience could be completely difference as far as different strategies for getting freebies are concerned. As such, you have to practice so that you can understand what works for you and what doesn't.

How To Hunt For High Quality Freebie Products and Services Online

There are a million and one ways to get free things. At the top of my mind, one of these ways is getting gifts from loved ones. But have you ever wondered whether there could actually be another way you could get free stuff? If you have, you're in luck because in this book, we shall focus on how to get high quality freebie products and services online.

This book will equip you with everything you need to go from a freebie-hunting novice to a freebie-hunting master who knows how to get the best high-end devices and services.

This book will give you free resources you can instantly use to snatch online freebies in an instance. It will also outline the steps you need to take to get freebies from your favorite companies.

If you're excited to get started, let's get right to it.

Everything You Need To Know About Freebie Products and Services Online

"The truly free man is the one who can turn down an invitation to dinner without giving an excuse."

- Jules Renard

The term "free" usually means different things to all of us. To some, it means getting something without paying for it. To others, it may mean getting a free sample gift at the local supermarket. Unfortunately, most of us are enormously cynical of the products we refer to as "free", and always look out for their hidden costs. For example, when you go to the local mart and a company-hired marketer offers to give you a gift, you're always quick to ask, "what's the catch?"

It's not hard to find out the origin of this cynicism. In business, free is not used in the same context as most of us interpret it. In fact, marketers use the 'science of freebies' to lure customers in. What type of freebies do you desire? Do you want freebies that have caveats to them? Or do you want freebies that have zero strings attached to them? My guess is that you fall in the latter category.

Now, I must say and point out that while there are many mega companies bustling to give you freebies, it is highly unlikely that you'll get to enjoy these gifts until you understand how freebies and freebies sites work. Let us do that now.

As indicated, most companies giving out freebies do so in the form of promotions and giveaways to consumers like you. Although the gifts present themselves as loyalty gifts, i.e. gifts you receive for "being loyal to the brand", the company giving this freebie expects to retain you as their client so that you can test other 'new' or 'old' products they may have and also so that you may market their products when and if you like them. In this case, the companies do not expect you to join their marketing team, no. They simply expect that since you like their product, and they have used a freebie of some sort to show you that you're a valued consumer, you will use word of mouth to recommend their products to your immediate circle.

These companies use the marketer's reciprocity principle. They use your sense of obligation to a good brand and the gifts they give you to motivate you to buy more and market them more.

Although this principle works extremely well for brick and motor companies with physical products, it also works extremely well for online products and services. However, for the online market, the idea has been tweaked and turned into freebie websites. What are freebies websites?

A freebie site is any directory or platform that lists free products that various companies have put up for grabs.

What you should note is that a freebie site does not give you free stuff; they merely give you information on what free product samples companies are offering. Freebie sites inform you as the visitor, what you need to do to claim the company's offer.

If you've been keen, you should have noted that when you click on a free sample link on most sites, that link redirects you to another site where you sign up for the freebie. This means, freebie sites are the third parties. They just direct you and leave the deal between you and advertising website. Think of them as messengers who find for you the companies giving out freebies and inform you about their freebies.

As you may have already guessed, there are many companies ready to offer you freebies. In fact, today, you can get high-end freebies such as gadgets, books, movies etc.

However, before you run out to start your freebie hunting adventure, you should know that even though thousands of companies offer gifts online and offline, the 'freebie industry' is not a free for all market. In fact, out of the thousands of people prospecting for high-end quality freebies, only a small percentage of them get the actual gifts.

I'm sure you're wondering, "what's so special about the small percentage that gets these freebies, or what it is that they do different so as to receive these gifts?"

The answer is simple: those who get freebies online are privy to some of the best principles and strategies you should follow and use to get freebies. Before we outline the strategies you can use to snag your high quality freebies, let us look at some guiding principles every 'freebie hunter' should follow.

The Three Freebie-Hunting Commandments

#1- Thou shall be pragmatic- Although the best things in life are free, don't quit your day job to become a full time online freebie prospector. Although you can get tons of free things online, it is very unlikely that the freebies will make you rich.

#2- Thou shall not sell your freebies online-When you succeed in getting free stuff, which you will, don't sell it for profit. Putting your freebies on craigslist or e-bay is equal to opening a can of legal worms.

#3- Thou shall be honest- When you receive a free product that you don't like, be decent enough not to recommend it to others.

Now that you have rules to follow as you prospect for online freebies, let us examine strategies that should guide your freebie-prospecting mission.

Freebie Scoring Strategies

There are many ways of scoring online freebies. Unfortunately, getting high quality freebies is not always easy. For example, CNET gets many high-end tech freebies; CNET is a technology review website. In fact, whenever a new technological device hits the market, they are usually the first ones to test it and write a comprehensive review about that product.

However, for them to get to where they are, they have had to do certain things. For example, CNET is a review website. Which means, for them to get to where they are, they have had to buy devices (they get them for free now, but they didn't always use to), test them and write a review that helps other people who may be interested in that particular device. That is CNET's strategy for scoring freebies. Let me ask you something; what is your freebie scoring strategy? Do you even have one?

The truth is that, until you formulate a strategy, there will be no difference between you and the thousands of people who have tried to score high-end freebies year in year out to no avail. You must create your strategy.

Your strategy will guide you to the freebies of your choice. Unless you're willing to put in the time and snag freebies the hard way, i.e. substitute your time for a high-end freebie (this is the same thing CNET did; they spend their time reviewing devices and writing reviews and in return, they get free high end tech devices). You need to create a strategy that guides you to where the freebies are instead of chasing the freebies all year round.

Your freebie strategy will depend on what types of freebies you desire and what you're willing to do to get them. To create your freebie strategy, follow the prompts below.

Keep your eyes and ears open.

You need to be well informed of all available freebie opportunities. Freebies won't just fall into your lap. In fact, if you know about Tom Locke and his $39 experiment(http://www.the39dollarexperiment.com/), you know that out of the many companies that offer freebies, only a few of them will offer you freebies. Don't' just sit around and wait for companies to send you emails or letters of the freebies they are offering. Stalk (in a good way) all your favorite companies on social media and in the news to know when these companies offer freebies to their loyal customers. Keep your eyes and ears open to any places that may be offering the freebies of your choice. For example, many radio stations often give out quality freebies for commenting, liking, and sharing their status updates on social media. At the same time, when Microsoft, Samsung or Apple announces new devices; there are tons of companies offering these devices for free.

Choose wisely

Before you sign the dotted line and opt in to a freebie, pay attention to the fine print. Look to see whether there are limitations or catches. Sometimes some offers are indeed too good to be true. Some companies may indicate that they're giving out a free TV or car but at the end of it they ask for your credit card and then charge you an exuberant shipping fee that to compensate them for the TV or car.

When most companies do their marketing, they tend to ask for your demographic information such as, medical condition, income, or size of household. Be cautious not to give out any personal information to them.

Create a secondary email address

Sometimes, companies give out birthday freebies or coupons to consumers who like them on social media or who are signed up for that company's mailing list. Fortunately, you can join as many company mailing lists as you want. However, to separate your emails; it's good practice to create a separate email account before signing up for any freebie online. This ensures that you only disclose the information you're comfortable with. It will also ensure that your freebie email alerts and important personal emails stay separate. Create one email account dedicated to any online freebie opt-in.

Act quickly

Many high quality freebies tend to be available on limited supply. Moreover, their availability is highly dependent on how fast the word spreads. Today, with the increased use of social media, word of high quality freebies spreads very fast. When you see high-end freebies, waste no time. Snatch them fast before someone else does.

Remember to have some fun

I assume you're not a professional freebie enthusiast. If you're not, remember not to get angry when you ask Channel to send you a free sample of their signature cologne and they flatly tell you to buy your own. It is highly unlikely that all the companies you email or ask to send you free samples will. Remember to have fun with this. When a company says "no", simply move on to the next one. There are thousands of companies just waiting for you to ask them for freebies.

*Key point/action step

The first step to getting any online freebie is a strategy. A strategy determines how you hunt for freebies. For example, you cannot hunt for a freebie you can't see. To snag high quality freebies, you need information. Where and how you get this information forms the crux of why you need a strategy. Fortunately, you now have everything you need to create a strategy.

How To Get Free Stuff From Amazon

"... You basically have a license to drive a Hummer through the Amazon"

- Thomas Friedman

Yes! Amazon is a free for all freebie market. If you're a frequent Amazon shopper, you've probably seen the thousands of users writing awesome positive reviews on products. Although most of these people are customers who've bought an item and left an informative review to help others, a big percentage of these people, i.e. the many people writing Amazon reviews do so in return for a free product.

In fact, at this particular moment, there are probably thousands of companies with Amazon store just baying for people to write them reviews in exchange for free sample gifts. This could be you today! You may be wondering why Amazon would want to give out free stuff. After all, they're in the business of making money, right? Well, the answer is simple: Amazon FBA.

Amazon has made it tremendously easy for anyone to sell products warehoused and shipped through their FBA program. Now, if we were to go back to our marketing knowledge, we know that in the online space, products with more reviews tend to outdo products with lesser reviews.

This is extremely good news for you because, on a daily basis, Amazon receives hundreds of new products to include in their fulfillment program. Most of these products can be yours through two ways:

Hard way

There are two ways to get things freely from Amazon; first is by being part of them. Amazon invites "vine voice" community members to contribute to reviews in exchange for gifts. If we're being honest, this way is not that ideal because you have to trade in your time and write a bunch of helpful reviews before they can even think about inviting you to their program.

That is the first way of getting Amazon to give you free stuff. The second way is the easy way...

Easy Way

Amazon has many digital nomads listing their products on the store. Most if not all of these companies use a service referred to as Tomoson(https://www.tomoson.com/about-tomoson/features) to find people i.e. normal people like you and me to whom they can send their free products to in exchange for some word of mouth hype.

Most of these companies often tend to give out a 100% off coupon code for their items, or ask you to buy their products and they reimburse you for it. Either way, all you need to do is to leave a review of these products and voila! That item is yours to keep, forever!

To get started, sign up for their account to get access to their products. After creating your account, link it with your social media account. After this, head over to blogger or WordPress and create a free blog to start writing reviews and sharing them on social media.

Coincidentally, every day, a ton of new Amazon review sites pop up everywhere. While you may have zero experience with them and the freebies they offer, they follow the Amazon concept. You should realize that every day, dozens of online sellers are willing to offer you their product freely if you're willing to write a review. In fact, some of them don't require a twitter or blog; just the Amazon review. Take advantage of this.

You probably may be wondering, "Why should I bother with Amazon?" Here is why. Although you have to trade in your time for a free product (writing the review), due to the sheer number of high end freebies available and the multi-national companies willing to give you their products in exchange for a review, Amazon is worth the effort. In fact, if you build a good website that has helpful reviews, Tomoson will not hesitate to give you the latest iPhone or Samsung Galaxy if they think it will give the phone some much needed social sharing.

*Key point/action step

Although it may not seem like it, thousands of people receive freebies from Amazon every day. All you have to do is sign up, choose your gift, receive it and write a comprehensive review geared to help people. Of course, the company wants a positive review. However, if there's something specific you hate about a product, make sure to point out in the product cons.

Get Companies To Send You Freebies

"We must free ourselves of the hope that the sea will ever rest. We must learn to sail in high winds."

- Aristotle Onassis

To get a company to send you free products, you must do something in return. They say that 'fortune favors the brave'. Although this may sound very far from our topic of discussion, to get companies to send you free stuff, you have to take broad steps such as joining rewards program, taking surveys, complaining about a product, or requesting free samples. In fact, getting companies to send you free stuff is that simple. All it requires is the following steps.

Method 1: Complain about a product

As a consumer, you have a right to complain about any product or service that has not met your demand. This is natural and something meant to guarantee equal treatment and services. You can also complain your way to free products. However, it is only best to complain about items, products, and services that fall short of their advertising glory. Complaining your way to free products does not mean becoming like the very famous British woman who rakes in 200 USD of products in a month by bombarding companies with complain mail concerning poor services and products. There is a right and a wrong way to complain to companies. Here is how to go about it

Step 1: Complain about a product you want

You cannot just pop out a deceitful complain and expect to receive a freebie just like that. You should have a reasonable complain that is worth compensation. For example;

If you're in a hotel where you're served a cup of coffee but notice a dead fly floating inside your mug of coffee, that is a complain worth compensating. The same principle applies to the online space. If an online service or product is below the standards you would expect in a related product, you have a right to complain and get reimbursed with a new free product.

Step 2: Locate the company's contact info

How are you going to reach out to the company you want to complain to? Are you going to reach out via email postal address, etc.? Fortunately, you can easily locate most company email addresses on their product packages. If this seems tedious, you can always go to that company's website.

Step 3: Communicate with the company

After getting the company's number or email address, contact them and let them know about your displeasure with a specific product. Include your proof of purchase in your complaint. Be persistent without being rude and ask them to replace the products by giving you a gift card

Step 4: Be patient

Keep calm and wait for your freebies. Most companies will placate you with a flattering replacement item or a redeemable voucher for a free item. Most companies will also reply to your mail to thank you for the continued support and input.

Method 2: Join rewards schemes

This is another simple way of wining yourself freebies. Most big companies have a reward team that rewards consumers for their royalty. Freebies on a reward scheme can sometimes be invaluable. Don't mind this. Make a point of finding out if your favorite company has a reward scheme you can join. Here is a systematic guide on how to rake it big with rewards schemes.

Step 1: Find rewards program

Members of a rewards team have access to product vouchers, coupons, discounts off on purchasing or points towards different prizes. After you find out if your company has a rewards team, join and enjoy the advantages.

Step 2: Join numerous programs

The more reward teams you join the more free items and discounts you'll get. For instance, if you join various grocery stores reward teams, one of them might be rewarding their consumers with free items today and another one tomorrow. This may place you at an advantage.

Step 3: Focus on one credit card rewards scheme

If a reward scheme is offering free credit cards to win points and redeem them for items, concentrate on a single card to increase your points. Doing this will maximize your points and thus maximize your point to free gift ratio.

Step 4: Redeem rewards before expiry

Most rewards have a limited life expectancy. You may intend to target the accumulation of points to a certain level before redeeming for a favored item only to discover that your points expired long before you could use them. Unless you are sure your rewards have no expiry date, always redeem them as soon as possible.

Method 3: Take surveys

Most people tend to think that taking surveys for freebies is not a cool or legit way of getting online freebies. Part of the reason for this is because there are many scam survey sites coning people of their hard earned cash. To ensure you don't fall prey to this bogus sites, follow the following steps.

Step 1: Keep your receipts

Most stores nowadays have a websites where consumers can complete surveys about shopping or dining experience. Their gifts in most cases are gift card or vouchers, a cash prize or a discount on your next shopping after completing the survey. If you visit most company websites, a pop up window may pop up prompting you to take a survey about your user experiences with that company. Don't hesitate to take the survey if the window promises to compensate your time with free stuffs or coupons.

Step 2: Get paid to take surveys

Most companies offer consumer surveys. The companies tend to do this to get product feedback and to advertise their products. You can find some of these companies online. In fact, there are thousands of legit online companies and websites offering cash for surveys. Ipsos survey panel(http://www.i-say.com/) is a very good example. Sign up and start taking their surveys. If they pick you to complete more in-depth surveys, you might end up receiving free items from various companies.

Method 4: Request free samples

You can get free samples from various companies depending on how you explain your need for the sample or how you choose to approach the company. Most well established companies give out their products samples to their consumers for product testing or for marketing purposes.

To win yourself free sample items, try this out;

Step 1: Write a letter to the company

When writing a letter to a company in the hope of snagging free samples, focus on telling them how their company and products rock. You can also try to tilt the odds of winning freebies by adding a personal experience story to the brand. For example, if you want a free product from a toy manufacturer, let them know you have used their products before and you loved their products. This will show the company that you know about their other products and have used them. The trick to pulling this off is being enthusiastic and specific as much as you can.

Request for free products by asking the company whether they have any free coupons or samples for their loyal consumers.

Step 2: Start a product review blog

If you write product's review for specific companies on your blog, asking that company to send you their free samples for review purposes is very easy. Most companies will give you free products for free publicity on your blog.

*Key point/action step

Truthfully, getting companies to send you products is not always easy. However, if you're persistent, take rejection with a pinch of sugar and a lot of goofiness, you will undoubtedly rake in those high quality freebies you've been searching for. The trick to getting companies to send you free stuff is by connecting with them on a personal level.

How To Score High Quality Freebies Online

"I know where I'm going and I know the truth, and I don't have to be what you want me to be. I'm free to be what I want"

- Muhammad Ali

They say chance favors the bold. By being bold, you can easily get free gadgets, entertainment, free travel, and even free internet access by knowing a few easy tips and tricks. Here are a few of these tips and tricks guaranteed to get you access to high quality freebies.

Gadgets

Almost all consumer gadgets are often in high demand. This makes it a bit difficult but not impossible to get high quality gadgets.

To receive free consumer electronic, you require a little bit of ingenuity. Nevertheless, it is important to keep your expectations in check. Getting free gadgets will require you to sacrifice some of your choices. For example, you may be focusing on an iPad as a freebie. While this is ok, it is not a feasible focus because often times, stores, or companies rarely ever give out the latest product. In fact, as you prospect for high-end free devices, you should note that often times, you would have to compromise and go for a lesser product model.

There are various ways to go about snagging high quality freebies. Here are a few of these ways

Write reviews

For years now, I've been exchanging reviews for high-end devices such as PlayStation, cell phones, etc. For me, it started with one Amazon review where after Amazon noted that my reviews helped many people on the site, they invited me to join a private program referred to as Vine.

Through this program, Amazon sends out a newsletter accompanied by new products offered by different companies to me every few weeks. Every member of Vine can claim any product for free as long as it is still available. In return, Vine members are required to write a review. This is something you can do today to get free books, gadgets and more. All you have to do is write helpful reviews. Fortunately, we've already looked at how to become a member of vine and get free things almost anytime you want to.

Appreciate and acquire the gadgets of the past

Everyone wants the latest gadgets. This makes them a bit difficult to come by in the freebie world. If you accept older tech items, such as old iPhones, you can always find them on sites such as, Craigslist and Freecycle(http://www.freecycle.com/). Everything on Freecycle is free. On craigslist, you will have to search for $0 items or search for terms such as "free" and "curb alert." You can also go to craigslist main page and click on the 'free' section. In addition, craigslist provides a web tool that alerts you whenever they have free gadgets.

How to acquire free movies, books and other media

If finding free gadgets appears to be tricky, finding free movies, books and other media happens to be simpler. It requires less of your work and gives you a fair number of choices. Below are your options:

Keep writing reviews

When you become a helpful online reviewer and gain access to Amazon Vine, you have at your disposal different ways to acquire free music, movies, and books. If you're looking for the best books, I suggest you try Google Good reads.

Find free books online

There are many free books online offered by "Google Books" in form of text and audio. There is an app called Kindle; if you install it in your device, you can get public domain books free from Amazon. All you need is to search and download whatever you want.

How To Stop Paying For Phone And Internet Services

Phone services and internet access should not cost you anything since you can get both free. All it takes you is signing up for the right services. Here are a few tips.

Acquire free broadband internet services with FreedomPop(https://www.freedompop.com/)

Accessing broadband internet tends to be expensive. However, with Freedom pop, it will cost you a deposit of $100, which you can get back after you cancel your service.

When you sign up for the service on your phone, it will turn your mobile into a Wifi hotspot that will provide reasonably data connection that is fast even when serving five computers through WiMAX network. By default, they offer you 500mb on a monthly basis. In case you complete your offer, you can earn extra data that is fantastic for casual browsing or on occasional on-the-go connection.

Make calls free to US and Canada using Gmail

As long as you can access the internet, you don't have to pay for your phone calls. Gmail offers free calling via Google voice to Cell phones and landlines between Canada and the United States. All you have to do is to create a Gmail account and have an active internet connection and you can talk as much as you want for free.

Travel free

Travelling is not cheap. However, by taking advantage of frequent flier programs and using a few tricks, you can knock down those entire travel costs. To travel free, you have to do bit of work, but almost everybody can earn discounts with minimal effort. Here are a few hacks to help you out:

Sign up for travel programs and reward cards at the right time

We all know that to earn frequent flier miles using credit cards that offer bonuses requires thousands of dollars and thousands of in-flight hours to earn a round trip flight. Delta or Star Alliance Airlines, have branded travel credit cards that offers you 25000-30000 points when you sign up and make one purchase. That's equals to free ticket.

To kick your mileage balance airline credit cards are the best. American airline offers 75000 miles after you purchase their branded credit card, Virgin Atlantic offers 50,000 and United offers 40000. Get one of these travel credit cards and gain free miles the best and quickest way.

*Key point/action step

It is crucial to remember that free isn't really free. You might not be paying with your money, but you are paying with information, effort or something else. In some cases, the sacrifices you make are worthwhile, but generally know what exactly you are sacrificing.

How to Apply What You've Learned?

At this particular moment, you have everything you need to start high end, quality freebies and services. However, remember that the type of freebies you get depends on your strategy. For example, to get the latest tech devices, your best bet is by going with reviewing your way to them. Remember: your freebie hunting strategy is very important. Create one adhering to the principles and commandments we listed in chapter one.

Amazon is a free for all freebie for those who know how to run through the freebie maze. Getting free stuff from Amazon requires reviews. The best thing about Amazon is their invitation only Vine program. The trick to being great at Amazon reviews is creating witty and honest reviews.

Every day, thousands of companies send freebies to their consumers. Getting companies to send you the item is not always easy, but with a clear contact strategy (preferably an enthusiastic message that paints you as the most enthusiastic consumer that company has), snagging freebies from companies is easy.

Unfortunately, free is not always free. When opting in to a free offer, make a point of reading the fine print. Know exactly what you're getting into before you get into it. After all, a bit of cynicism never hurt anyone.

www.ingramcontent.com/pod-product-compliance
Lightning Source LLC
LaVergne TN
LVHW011102240225
804411LV00009B/647